Contents

1 Introduction to Welfare Assistance

Welfare assistance, at its core, is about supporting individuals and families in need. It's a complex system, involving a vast network of agencies, programs, and the dedicated individuals who navigate this landscape daily. Understanding the current structure, its challenges, and its potential is the first step towards building a more effective and supportive system. We must acknowledge the inherent complexities involved in resource allocation, policy implementation, and the human element of providing assistance. Successful navigation requires a keen understanding of the legal framework, ethical considerations, and the socio-economic factors impacting those who rely on these services.

The individuals who form the backbone of welfare assistance – the workforce – are incredibly diverse. They are caseworkers, social workers, administrators, and countless others, each contributing in unique ways to this crucial system. Many work tirelessly to connect individuals with vital resources. Their roles vary significantly, depending on the specific agency and program, but they share a common goal: to help those in need. The sheer breadth of responsibilities requires a workforce with a diverse skillset, able to handle complex situations with empathy, efficiency, and a deep understanding of the challenges faced by those they serve. This necessitates a robust training infrastructure.

Many welfare agencies grapple with staffing shortages and high turnover rates. These challenges often stem from a lack of adequate training, limited career progression opportunities, and insufficient compensation. Addressing these issues requires a multi-pronged approach focusing not only on immediate needs but also on long-term workforce development strategies. Effective planning requires accurate data collection and analysis to truly understand the current needs and anticipate future challenges. This will help inform effective training strategies.

Effective training should be more than just a series of lectures; it should be engaging and relevant to the daily realities of the job. Interactive workshops, simulations, and on-the-job mentoring can significantly enhance learning and retention. The curriculum must reflect the needs of the workforce, incorporating both technical skills and the crucial soft skills like empathy, communication, and conflict resolution. This approach requires a collaborative effort between training providers, welfare agencies, and those in the field, ensuring the curriculum accurately reflects the reality of the job.

Creating clear career pathways is essential for retaining experienced staff and attracting new talent. These pathways must provide opportunities for advancement, professional development, and increased responsibility. Mentorship programs, where experienced workers guide newer staff, are particularly valuable, helping to pass on critical knowledge and build a supportive workplace culture. Offering opportunities for specialized training, advanced certifications, or even pursuing higher education can motivate staff and attract top talent while fostering a more engaged and proficient workforce. Investing in the workforce benefits everyone.

Implementing these changes requires a commitment to sustained funding and ongoing evaluation. Regular program assessments allow for improvements and adaptations to ensure the training remains effective and relevant. Collaboration across different agencies is key, ensuring efficiency and consistency in service delivery. Open communication is crucial, fostering a supportive environment where new ideas and best practices can be shared effectively. Regular collaboration meetings should be incorporated to facilitate this. This continuous improvement loop allows for the greatest adaptability and efficacy.

Ultimately, building a strong and capable welfare workforce is an investment in a more resilient and effective system. It is not merely about addressing immediate needs but about fostering a sustainable future for those who depend on welfare assistance and those who provide it. This is a long-term commitment that requires collaboration, innovation, and a dedication to providing comprehensive support to the entire system, ensuring it is prepared to meet the ever-evolving needs of society. The payoff, in improved services and a more supportive system, will be invaluable.

1.1 The Current Landscape

The welfare system, a crucial societal safety net, faces significant challenges. A primary concern is the workforce itself; often under-resourced, under-trained, and facing high turnover rates. This directly impacts the quality of service provided to vulnerable populations. Effective service delivery necessitates a skilled, motivated, and well-supported workforce. Without adequate training and career development opportunities, the system's ability to meet the evolving needs of its beneficiaries is compromised. The current landscape reveals a disparity between the skills possessed by current employees and the skills needed for optimal performance. This gap needs to be addressed urgently and proactively.

This mismatch isn't simply about lacking specific technical skills; it's also about a broader deficiency in crucial soft skills. Effective communication, empathy, case management expertise, and the ability to navigate complex bureaucratic systems are all vital. Many caseworkers are burdened by heavy workloads and lack the necessary resources to effectively serve clients. Training must address these multifaceted needs, going beyond simple technical instruction to foster holistic professional development. Furthermore, the current system often lacks robust mechanisms for ongoing professional development. Continuous learning and adaptation are vital in a constantly evolving social landscape, yet opportunities for professional enrichment are often limited, contributing to staff burnout and attrition.

Many welfare agencies rely heavily on outdated training methods and lack the resources to invest in modern technology and innovative training approaches. Online learning platforms, simulations, and interactive workshops can enhance learning and improve knowledge retention. Effective training isn't simply a one-time event; it's an ongoing process of development and refinement. A well-structured training program should consist of various modules, addressing both fundamental skills and specialized areas of expertise. Modular training allows for flexibility and enables agencies to tailor training to individual needs and the specific demands of their clients. Regular assessments should be integrated to

gauge the effectiveness of the training and identify any gaps needing immediate attention. Importantly, these assessment methods should go beyond traditional tests and include practical application exercises to ensure real-world competency.
Creating clear career pathways is equally vital for retaining talent. A stagnant career structure often leads to disenchantment and high turnover. Offering opportunities for advancement, specialized training, and leadership development will enhance job satisfaction and motivate employees to remain in the field. Implementing mentorship programs and fostering a supportive work environment will help nurture talent and promote long-term growth. A successful program doesn't just offer better training; it creates a dynamic system where welfare workers are valued, supported, and empowered to make a real difference in the lives of others. It fosters a sense of community and collaboration, enabling workers to share best practices, and build a shared understanding of challenges and solutions.
Addressing the current landscape requires a comprehensive strategy. It's not enough to simply identify the problems; we must develop sustainable solutions that promote a more skilled, well-supported, and engaged welfare workforce. This requires investment in better training, improved career development opportunities, and the creation of a supportive work environment that values the contributions of welfare workers. Addressing these issues will lead to improved service delivery, better outcomes for vulnerable populations, and a more robust and resilient welfare system capable of meeting the challenges of the future. The creation of robust, data-driven systems for monitoring and evaluating the effectiveness of training programs is crucial. This includes measuring not only knowledge acquisition but also changes in work

performance and client outcomes. By systematically analyzing program impact, we can continuously refine our training approaches and ensure they align with the evolving needs of the welfare system. This requires collaboration between agencies, researchers, and policymakers to establish clear benchmarks, and develop tools to accurately track and interpret data.

Ultimately, a thriving welfare workforce depends on a system that values its employees. This includes competitive salaries and benefits, fair working conditions, and opportunities for growth and advancement. A robust system of professional development is not just an investment in employees; it's an investment in the well-being of the communities they serve. By prioritizing the needs of the workforce, we can create a more effective, equitable, and sustainable welfare system that effectively addresses the needs of vulnerable individuals and families. This includes supporting ongoing research to identify emerging needs and trends within the field and fostering ongoing dialogue between policymakers, practitioners, and researchers to ensure the welfare system remains responsive to the evolving needs of society. Collaboration is key in building a system where all stakeholders are committed to improving the welfare of the workforce and the communities it serves. A stronger welfare system will improve lives, reduce poverty, and contribute to a more equitable society.

1.2 Defining Welfare's Workforce

The welfare workforce is incredibly diverse. It includes not only caseworkers directly interacting with clients, but also supervisors, administrators, data analysts, IT specialists, and even legal professionals who navigate the complexities of welfare law. Each role, while distinct, contributes to the overarching goal of providing essential support and services. Understanding this multifaceted nature is fundamental to addressing the challenges and opportunities within the system. We need to move beyond simplistic definitions and acknowledge the intricate web of skills, experiences, and responsibilities that underpin this crucial sector. Effective training and career development must reflect this complexity, acknowledging the unique needs of each role and fostering collaboration across different disciplines. We must also consider the emotional toll that working within welfare assistance can take, requiring robust support systems and attention to mental well-being.

Effective service delivery hinges on a well-trained and motivated workforce. This isn't simply about possessing technical skills; it's about cultivating empathy, cultural competence, and a deep understanding of the social determinants of health and poverty. Caseworkers, for instance, need strong communication skills to build rapport with clients, navigate sensitive situations, and effectively explain complex procedures. They also require strong critical thinking abilities to assess individual needs, determine eligibility for programs, and develop personalized support plans. Administrative staff, meanwhile, must possess organizational skills, proficiency in various software programs, and a keen eye for detail to ensure the smooth operation of the welfare system. Data analysts must be able to interpret complex datasets and make evidence-based recommendations for improved program effectiveness. The diverse skillsets required highlight the need for a tailored approach to training and development, recognizing the varying demands across different roles.

Training programs must extend beyond basic skill-building

and incorporate ongoing professional development. This includes regular updates on policy changes, new technologies, and best practices in social work and case management. It's also vital to offer opportunities for mentorship and peer learning, creating a supportive environment where staff can share experiences, learn from each other, and build professional networks. These ongoing development opportunities are essential for retaining experienced staff and preventing burnout. Continuous learning is not a mere suggestion; rather, it's a necessity in a field where policies, regulations, and the needs of the clients are constantly evolving. Providing regular training is not just an investment in the workforce; it's an investment in the effectiveness and sustainability of the welfare system itself.

Career pathways within the welfare system should be clearly defined and accessible to all employees. This means creating a structured progression of roles, with opportunities for advancement based on performance, experience, and professional development. This system needs to not only provide clear steps for employees to advance, but should also create a culture of growth and achievement within the workforce. By offering clearly defined career paths, we can encourage staff retention, increase motivation, and attract new talent. This strategic approach also acknowledges that the work done is meaningful and valuable, and offers a clear path for staff who might otherwise leave welfare work for more advanced opportunities. This systematic approach is crucial to retain the experienced and dedicated professionals already working in the welfare sector.

Creating a supportive work environment is equally important. Welfare work can be emotionally demanding, requiring staff to deal with challenging situations and the often-complex needs of vulnerable populations. Therefore, the system needs to provide adequate resources such as robust supervision, employee assistance programs, and opportunities for self-care. Investing in employee well-being isn't just a matter of compassion; it's a strategy to improve staff retention, reduce burnout, and ultimately, enhance the quality of service delivery. The wellbeing of the workforce directly reflects the quality of service provided to individuals in need. This ensures that staff are not only equipped to do their jobs, but also protected from the emotional strain inherent in the field.

Finally, effective recruitment strategies are crucial to attract a diverse and skilled workforce to the welfare sector. This involves actively reaching out to potential candidates from a variety of backgrounds, emphasizing the value of the work, and creating a welcoming and inclusive organizational culture. Competitive salaries, comprehensive benefits packages, and attractive working conditions are equally important to attracting top talent and retaining seasoned professionals. We must also combat the misconceptions and stigma surrounding the field, promoting welfare work as a rewarding and impactful career choice for professionals committed to making a difference in the lives of others. This active and strategic recruitment strategy will ensure the long-term viability of the welfare workforce.

2 Identifying Skills Gaps

Pinpointing skill deficiencies within welfare assistance requires a multifaceted approach. We must move beyond simple observation and employ rigorous assessment methods. This involves utilizing standardized tests, comprehensive surveys, and targeted interviews to gather data on existing skill levels and identify areas needing improvement. Equally crucial is analyzing employee performance reviews, identifying recurring shortcomings in service delivery. The goal is not just to identify weaknesses, but to understand the root causes—are these gaps due to insufficient initial training, a lack of ongoing professional development, or perhaps systemic issues within the welfare system itself? A thorough understanding of these underlying factors will guide the development of effective interventions.

Effective data analysis is paramount. This isn't simply about compiling numbers; it's about interpreting trends and drawing meaningful conclusions. For example, are we seeing consistent deficits in specific areas such as case management or financial literacy? Are there regional disparities in skill levels, hinting at the need for localized training initiatives? Advanced statistical techniques, like regression analysis, can help unravel complex relationships and pinpoint areas requiring immediate attention. Visualizing this data through graphs and charts can make complex information easily accessible to decision-makers, fostering a shared understanding of the challenges at hand and driving informed policy decisions. The aim should always be to translate raw data into actionable insights, paving the way for targeted improvements.

Addressing specific needs demands a nuanced approach, tailored to the unique challenges identified during the assessment phase. We can't adopt a one-size-fits-all mentality. For instance, if the data reveals a widespread deficiency in understanding complex regulations, the solution might involve creating specialized training modules focused on legal interpretation. Conversely, a lack of technological proficiency might necessitate training programs focused on specific software applications relevant to case management or data analysis. These training programs must be interactive, engaging, and easily accessible to welfare professionals, perhaps utilizing both online and in-person training modalities to cater to diverse learning styles. Regular feedback mechanisms are also essential to ensure the training programs effectively address the identified skill gaps.

Beyond individual skills, we must consider the overall organizational context. A supportive workplace culture that prioritizes professional development is crucial. This might involve creating mentorship programs, where experienced staff guide and support new recruits. Regular supervision sessions should incorporate constructive feedback and opportunities for skill enhancement. Furthermore, fostering a culture of continuous learning encourages welfare professionals to proactively seek opportunities to improve their skills, ultimately contributing to better service delivery. A commitment to professional development will not only improve individual

capabilities, but create a more dynamic and engaged workforce. This, in turn, fosters a sense of professional pride and career satisfaction, increasing employee retention.
The success of any initiative hinges on effective communication and collaboration. This means actively involving welfare professionals in the identification and prioritization of training needs. Their input is invaluable, as they possess first-hand experience with the daily challenges of service delivery. Transparency is crucial; open communication about the assessment process, the resulting data, and the planned interventions will foster buy-in and support. Successful strategies often involve partnering with external organizations and educational institutions, leveraging their expertise and resources to augment internal capacity. This collaborative approach facilitates resource sharing, avoids duplication of efforts, and ensures a comprehensive approach to skill development. Active participation from all stakeholders will pave the way to sustained improvements in welfare service delivery.

2.1 Assessment Methods

Understanding the skills and knowledge possessed by welfare workers is crucial. This necessitates a multifaceted approach to assessment, moving beyond simple questionnaires to encompass a range of methods that provide a comprehensive picture. We need to consider individual worker capabilities, the needs of the population served, and the evolving demands of the welfare system itself. A robust assessment strategy will be critical in informing targeted training and career development initiatives, ensuring that the welfare workforce is equipped to meet the challenges of today and tomorrow. This isn't simply about ticking boxes; it's about creating a dynamic and responsive system.

One crucial method is performance-based assessment. This involves observing workers in their actual work environment, analyzing their approach to client interactions, their ability to manage caseloads effectively, and their adherence to best practices. Structured observation protocols, using predefined criteria and rating scales, ensure objectivity and consistency. This method allows for the identification of both strengths and weaknesses, leading to individualized training plans. Furthermore, observations can be complemented by interviews with supervisors and peers to gain a holistic understanding of an individual's performance and potential. This provides a rich data set, allowing for nuanced evaluation, and avoiding the pitfalls of relying solely on self-reported data.

Self-assessment tools, such as questionnaires and surveys, offer a valuable perspective. These tools allow workers to reflect on their skills and identify areas for improvement. However, they must be carefully designed to avoid bias and ensure accuracy. Multiple-choice questions can be supplemented by open-ended questions that allow for more nuanced responses. Furthermore, the anonymity of self-assessment can encourage honest self-reflection, uncovering hidden skill deficits that might not be apparent through other methods. The design must also consider the literacy levels of the participants and use clear and concise language to ensure accurate comprehension and response. It's crucial to remember that while self-assessment provides valuable insights, it's most effective when combined with other assessment methods for a more complete picture.

Skill gap analysis goes beyond individual assessments; it requires examining the needs of the entire welfare workforce.

Data analysis, discussed in a later chapter, plays a pivotal role here, revealing systemic deficiencies. This data should identify specific skill gaps that affect service delivery, hindering the workforce's ability to efficiently and effectively support clients. For example, data might show a significant gap in knowledge of a specific piece of legislation or a lack of proficiency in a particular technology used for case management. Identifying these areas allows for the creation of targeted training that directly addresses the needs of the organization and ultimately, the clients they serve. This ensures resources are used efficiently, and training is relevant and impactful.

In addition to performance-based and self-assessment methods, 360-degree feedback provides a comprehensive evaluation. This approach involves collecting feedback from multiple sources, including supervisors, peers, subordinates, and even clients, offering a well-rounded perspective on an individual's strengths and weaknesses. It is crucial that feedback mechanisms are in place to encourage constructive criticism without fostering an environment of negativity or judgment. Gathering 360-degree feedback may also require sensitivity training for those giving and receiving feedback to ensure clear and constructive communication, thereby providing more comprehensive and meaningful results. This methodology can expose blind spots that may not be apparent through other methods, offering valuable insights into an individual's effectiveness and areas that need improvement. The incorporation of this feedback adds another layer of comprehensive evaluation, going beyond individual and supervisory evaluations to provide a complete picture.

Finally, it's essential to remember that assessment methods should be adaptable and responsive to changing needs. The welfare system is dynamic, with evolving legislation, emerging technologies, and changing client demographics constantly influencing the skillset required of its workforce. Regular review and updating of assessment tools and procedures are necessary to ensure they remain relevant and effective in identifying and addressing skill gaps. This means creating a feedback loop to capture the challenges faced during implementation and using this information to adapt assessment methods. This iterative approach ensures ongoing accuracy and alignment with the evolving needs of the workforce and the clients they serve, thereby maintaining the effectiveness of training initiatives and professional development programs.

2.2 Data Analysis & Trends

Analyzing data reveals crucial trends in the welfare workforce's skill sets. We find a significant disparity between the skills currently possessed by welfare professionals and the skills needed for optimal service delivery. For instance, proficiency in data analysis and technology is often lacking, hindering the effective use of available resources and the implementation of evidence-based practices. This gap is particularly pronounced in smaller agencies, where resources for training and professional development may be limited. The lack of training impacts client outcomes, as caseworkers may struggle to efficiently manage cases, access relevant resources, and navigate increasingly complex eligibility criteria. Therefore, investing in effective training programs becomes not just a matter of professional development, but directly impacts the quality of services offered to vulnerable populations.

This lack of technological proficiency, combined with insufficient knowledge of relevant social services and regulations, results in longer processing times and increased administrative burdens. Moreover, the data shows a higher rate of staff turnover in positions requiring advanced technical skills, suggesting these are difficult to fill due to a lack of qualified applicants. We must address this shortage proactively, as it significantly affects service efficiency and the overall effectiveness of the welfare system. A comprehensive solution will require a multi-pronged approach addressing training, recruitment, and career development within the field. We can improve access to continuing education opportunities. Such improvements could potentially resolve the shortage of skilled workers and improve the quality of care given to clients. This highlights a crucial need for targeted training initiatives and educational programs designed to equip welfare professionals with the necessary skills to use technology effectively in their roles.

Addressing these skill gaps requires a targeted approach, focusing not just on technical skills but also on critical thinking, problem-solving, and effective communication. This demands a significant shift in the way training programs are designed and implemented. We need to move beyond traditional, lecture-based training and incorporate active learning methodologies, such as simulations, case studies, and mentorship programs. Furthermore, training materials must be accessible and adaptable to accommodate various learning styles and technological proficiency levels. This ensures effective learning and development for everyone, including those with limited prior experience with technology.

Furthermore, current data indicates a pronounced lack of diversity within the welfare workforce, mirroring broader societal disparities. This impacts the ability of the system to effectively serve diverse populations and understand the unique challenges faced by marginalized communities. Addressing this issue requires proactive recruitment strategies and mentorship opportunities targeted toward underrepresented groups. These initiatives should strive to create an inclusive work environment that fosters professional development, retention, and advancement for all employees, regardless of their background or identity. We can use data analysis to identify areas for improvement and to measure the success of our initiatives.

Our analysis reveals a strong correlation between career development opportunities and staff retention rates. Creating clear career pathways, with opportunities for advancement and increased responsibility, is crucial for motivating employees and fostering a sense of professional fulfillment. Investing in these pathways not only strengthens the workforce but also improves the long-term stability and effectiveness of the welfare system. This requires a collaborative effort between welfare agencies, educational institutions, and professional organizations to develop robust training programs, create mentorship opportunities, and establish clear career ladders.

The analysis of existing data presents a compelling case for the need for systemic change. Simply offering sporadic training sessions is insufficient; a comprehensive, ongoing strategy is essential. This strategy must include not only initial training but also continuous professional development opportunities to ensure welfare staff remain up-to-date on best practices, emerging technologies, and policy changes. Agencies should prioritize funding for professional development activities and create incentives for staff to participate. This would improve staff morale and create a more motivated, effective workforce. This necessitates a long-term commitment from government agencies, private organizations and welfare providers to invest in the welfare workforce. This includes providing adequate funding for training programs, recruitment efforts and professional development initiatives.

Looking forward, integrating technology more effectively is essential. Data analysis and management skills are becoming increasingly crucial in the delivery of welfare services, demanding that training programs incorporate these areas into their curricula. This isn't just about learning software; it involves developing analytical skills to interpret data, identify trends, and make informed decisions. This requires a shift in mindset, moving from traditional casework approaches toward more data-driven strategies. This shift will benefit caseworkers and clients alike, as the information gleaned through effective data use will promote more efficient and effective service delivery.

In conclusion, the data clearly points to the need for a multifaceted strategy to address skill gaps and improve career pathways within the welfare workforce. This includes a dedicated focus on technological proficiency, addressing diversity issues, creating clear career ladders, and investing in comprehensive, ongoing training programs. By implementing these recommendations, we can strengthen the welfare system, enhance service delivery, and ultimately improve the lives of those who rely on it. This necessitates a sustained commitment from all stakeholders – policymakers, administrators, welfare professionals, and advocacy groups – to collaborate effectively and ensure the well-being and effectiveness of the welfare workforce. Only a comprehensive, coordinated effort can bridge the existing gaps and create a robust, equitable welfare system for the future.

2.3 Addressing Specific Needs

Understanding the specific needs of the welfare workforce requires a nuanced approach. We can't simply assume a one-size-fits-all solution. Instead, we need to delve into the individual requirements of different roles and responsibilities within the system. Caseworkers, for instance, need strong interpersonal skills, empathy, and a deep understanding of social work principles. Their training should focus on active listening techniques, conflict resolution strategies, and ethical considerations specific to vulnerable populations. Simultaneously, administrative staff require proficiency in data management, budgeting, and program coordination. Their training should emphasize software applications, financial literacy, and efficient workflow management. A tailored approach ensures that training aligns perfectly with each individual's unique job function.

The geographical location also plays a crucial role in determining specific training needs. A caseworker in a rural setting, for instance, might face different challenges compared to their urban counterpart. They may need extra training in transportation logistics, managing larger caseloads with limited resources, and working effectively within tight-knit communities where confidentiality is paramount. Conversely, an urban caseworker might require skills in navigating complex social networks, addressing issues of homelessness and urban poverty, and cooperating with a range of community organizations. Considering these diverse contexts, geographically-focused training modules could prove incredibly beneficial.

Beyond job function and location, personal learning styles and prior experiences must be taken into account. Some individuals learn best through hands-on training, while others prefer theoretical learning. Some may benefit from traditional classroom settings, whereas others thrive in online or blended learning environments. Acknowledging these different learning preferences is vital to ensure the effectiveness of any training initiative. Furthermore, the prior experience and educational background of welfare workers profoundly influence their training needs. Individuals with previous social work experience, for example, would require a different level of training compared to those entering the field for the first time. Adaptable training methodologies that cater to a range of experience levels are critical.

Incorporating technology into the training process is essential to enhance engagement and accessibility. Online learning platforms can offer flexibility and cost-effectiveness, allowing staff to access training materials at their convenience. Interactive simulations can recreate realistic scenarios, allowing trainees to practice their skills in a safe environment and receive immediate feedback. Integrating technology with traditional classroom instruction offers a blended learning approach, benefiting various learners and enhancing their overall understanding and skills retention. This modern approach to training is both essential and efficient in effectively meeting the requirements of a diverse workforce.

Furthermore, addressing the specific needs of the welfare workforce also requires considering the evolving nature of the field itself. Policy changes, emerging social issues, and advancements in technology consistently reshape the roles and responsibilities of welfare professionals. Regular updates to training curricula ensure staff possess the most current knowledge and skills to effectively serve the populations they support. This requires ongoing collaboration between training providers, policymakers, and welfare professionals themselves, ensuring that training remains relevant, responsive, and reflective of the ever-changing landscape of social services. These continuous training updates maintain a high level of workforce efficacy and responsiveness to community needs. A static training program cannot cater to a continuously evolving social landscape.

Moreover, the assessment of specific needs should not be a one-time event. Regular feedback mechanisms, such as surveys, focus groups, and performance reviews, are essential for identifying ongoing training needs and evaluating the impact of training programs. This continuous feedback loop ensures that training resources remain aligned with the actual needs of the workforce, thereby optimizing their effectiveness and improving the quality of service delivery to vulnerable populations. Regular assessment of individual needs and program outcomes allows for continual growth and refinement of training techniques. The field of welfare assistance demands adaptability and continual improvement.

Finally, remember that addressing specific needs isn't just about training; it's about creating a supportive and inclusive work environment. This includes providing access to mentorship programs, career development opportunities, and mental health resources. A well-supported workforce is a more engaged and effective workforce. Burnout is a serious concern within welfare professions; therefore, fostering a supportive environment that addresses the overall wellbeing of staff is not only ethical but also essential for maintaining service quality and staff retention. A comprehensive approach that addresses both training and wellbeing creates a robust and supportive workforce.

3 Effective Training Programs

Designing effective training programs requires a multifaceted approach. It's not simply about creating a curriculum; it's about building a comprehensive system that addresses individual learning styles, organizational needs, and the ever-evolving demands of the welfare system. We must consider the diverse backgrounds and experiences of the welfare workforce, ensuring that training is accessible, engaging, and relevant to their daily roles. A one-size-fits-all approach simply won't suffice. Success hinges on creating a learning environment that fosters collaboration, promotes critical thinking, and encourages continuous professional development.

Program delivery is equally crucial. A well-designed curriculum is useless without effective methods for its dissemination. This might involve a blend of in-person workshops, online modules, mentoring programs, and on-the-job training. The ideal approach often depends on the specific skill being taught, the learning styles of the participants, and the resources available. For example, technical skills may be best taught through hands-on workshops and simulations, while soft skills, such as communication and empathy, might benefit from role-playing exercises and group discussions. Flexibility and adaptability are key to successful program delivery. Continuously evaluating and adjusting the delivery method based on feedback and learner outcomes ensures the program remains effective and engaging.

Measuring program success goes beyond simply tracking completion rates. We need robust evaluation methods that assess the impact of training on individual performance, team effectiveness, and ultimately, the quality of services provided to clients. This necessitates the development of clear learning objectives and performance indicators at the outset of the program. Data collection methods should include pre\item and post-training assessments, performance reviews, and feedback from both trainees and supervisors. Analyzing this data allows us to identify areas of strength and weakness, helping us refine our training programs over time and ensure that they are delivering the desired results. Qualitative data, such as feedback from participants and supervisors, provides rich insights into the effectiveness and relevance of the training.

Securing adequate funding and resources is paramount for developing and sustaining effective training programs. This requires a multifaceted strategy, involving securing grants from government agencies and private foundations, as well as advocating for increased budgetary allocations within welfare organizations. Identifying and leveraging existing resources, such as free online training platforms and partnerships with universities and community colleges, can also help stretch limited budgets. Building a strong case for investment in training programs often involves demonstrating a clear return on investment through improved employee performance, reduced turnover, and ultimately, better service delivery for clients. This also includes considering the long-term costs and benefits of training initiatives to ensure financial sustainability.

Successful training programs rarely operate in isolation. They thrive on partnerships and collaboration between different organizations and stakeholders. This could involve collaborations with other government agencies, private sector organizations, educational institutions, and community-based groups. Such partnerships can provide access to diverse expertise, resources, and networks, expanding the reach and impact of training programs. For example, partnerships with employers can facilitate on-the-job training opportunities and create pathways for career advancement. Similarly, collaborations with educational institutions can help develop and update training curricula to align with current best practices and emerging industry standards. These collaborative efforts are essential for creating a robust and sustainable training ecosystem that supports the ongoing professional development of the welfare workforce.

3.1 Curriculum Design

Developing a robust curriculum for welfare assistance training requires a multifaceted approach. We must move beyond simple skill acquisition and foster critical thinking, problem-solving, and ethical decision-making. The curriculum should integrate real-world case studies, encouraging learners to apply theoretical knowledge to practical scenarios. Role-playing exercises and simulations can provide valuable experience in handling complex situations, preparing them for the emotional and logistical demands of the job. Furthermore, incorporating feedback mechanisms throughout the training process, from peer reviews to instructor evaluations, ensures continuous improvement and adaptation to the evolving needs of the field. Emphasis should be placed on developing cultural competency, understanding the diverse backgrounds and needs of the populations they serve.

Effective curriculum design begins with a thorough needs assessment. This involves analyzing data from multiple sources, including job descriptions, performance reviews, and feedback from both service recipients and welfare staff themselves. Identifying specific skill gaps is crucial for tailoring the curriculum's content and ensuring its relevance. For instance, if data reveals a deficiency in understanding specific regulations or handling sensitive client information, modules addressing these areas should be prioritized. This ensures that the training directly addresses the most pressing needs of the workforce and enhances their overall competence. The assessment should also consider emerging trends and technological advancements in the field, anticipating future skill requirements.

The structure of the curriculum should prioritize a blended learning approach, combining online modules with in-person workshops and practical training sessions. Online platforms offer flexibility and accessibility, allowing participants to learn at their own pace. In-person sessions, on the other hand, foster collaboration, networking opportunities, and direct interaction with instructors and peers. This blended approach caters to diverse learning styles and ensures a comprehensive learning experience. For example, a module focusing on interviewing techniques could involve online theoretical instruction supplemented by in-person role-playing sessions and feedback from experienced professionals. This interactive strategy boosts confidence and competence among trainees.

To maximize engagement and retention, the curriculum should employ various teaching methods. Lectures should be interspersed with interactive exercises, group discussions, and real-life case studies. Visual aids, such as videos and interactive simulations, can enhance understanding and make the learning process more dynamic. The integration of technology, like online learning platforms and interactive tools, can further enhance engagement and make the training more accessible. For instance, using virtual reality scenarios to simulate client interactions can provide invaluable, risk-free practice for trainees. Incorporating diverse learning styles and methods is key to creating an inclusive and effective training program.

Finally, the curriculum should be regularly evaluated and updated to reflect changes in the welfare landscape. Collecting feedback from participants, instructors, and supervisors is essential for identifying areas of strength and weakness. Data on program effectiveness, such as improvements in job performance and client satisfaction, should be rigorously analyzed to inform curriculum revisions. This ongoing evaluation process ensures that the training remains relevant, effective, and responsive to the evolving needs of the welfare workforce, contributing to a continuous improvement cycle. This iterative process guarantees that the training program remains a valuable and dynamic tool in enhancing the skills and competence of welfare professionals. The resulting curriculum empowers a workforce capable of delivering high-quality, effective, and compassionate service.

3.2 Program Delivery

Effective program delivery hinges on a multifaceted approach, moving beyond simple classroom instruction. Consider the context: welfare caseworkers often juggle demanding caseloads and emotional complexities. Therefore, training must be flexible, accessible, and responsive to their unique needs. Modular training, delivered both online and in person, allows for customized learning paths, catering to individual skill levels and time constraints. This blended learning model maximizes accessibility while ensuring comprehensive skill development. Furthermore, incorporating real-world case studies and simulations provides valuable practical experience, strengthening their ability to apply theoretical knowledge to everyday challenges.

Micro-learning techniques, focusing on short, targeted learning modules, improve retention rates and cater to busy schedules. These bite-sized units can be easily integrated into existing workloads, minimizing disruption. We need to move beyond the traditional lecture-style delivery; interactive workshops, peer-to-peer learning sessions, and mentoring opportunities foster collaboration and critical thinking. Regular feedback mechanisms, including peer and self-assessments, help track progress, identify areas for improvement, and sustain motivation. Such an approach acknowledges the crucial role of continuous learning and professional growth in this demanding field.

Successful program delivery also demands a commitment to ongoing support. Mentorship programs, pairing experienced caseworkers with newer staff, offer valuable guidance and practical support. This structured approach helps foster a supportive work environment and encourage professional development. Furthermore, providing access to updated resources, such as online databases, journals, and professional development webinars, keeps staff current on emerging trends and best practices within the field. This commitment to ongoing support is critical for retention and promoting a culture of continuous learning. Regular check-ins, performance reviews, and opportunities for professional feedback contribute to this crucial ongoing support system. It's not just about the initial training; it's a long-term investment in the workforce.

Beyond technical skills, effective program delivery must address the emotional toll inherent in welfare work. Burnout is a significant concern in this field; proactive strategies are crucial. Therefore, incorporate stress management techniques and emotional intelligence training into the curriculum. Providing access to mental health resources, including employee assistance programs and counseling services, displays a genuine commitment to employee well-being. Creating a supportive, understanding, and collaborative work environment is equally essential. A culture that values work-life balance and prioritizes employee well-being ultimately improves morale, retention rates, and the overall quality of service delivery.

Finally, measuring program effectiveness is essential for continuous improvement. Utilize a multi-faceted evaluation strategy, combining quantitative and qualitative data. Track key metrics such as skill acquisition, job performance, employee satisfaction, and client outcomes. Regular feedback from both trainees and supervisors can identify strengths and areas needing improvement, allowing for ongoing adjustments. Using this data to inform future training initiatives shows a commitment to program refinement and guarantees that the training remains relevant and effective. Such a continuous improvement cycle ensures the program's long-term sustainability and adaptability to evolving needs and challenges. Only through constant monitoring and improvement can we truly empower welfare's workforce to provide the most effective support.

3.3 Measuring Program Success

Measuring program success isn't simply about numbers; it's about understanding the impact on individuals' lives and the overall effectiveness of the welfare system. We need to move beyond simple metrics like completion rates and delve into the nuanced changes achieved. A truly successful program demonstrably enhances the skills and capabilities of welfare workers, leading to improved service delivery and better outcomes for those they serve. This requires a multi-faceted approach, incorporating both quantitative and qualitative measures.

Quantitative data, such as pre\item and post-training assessments, can measure the improvement in specific skills. For instance, we might track increases in knowledge of relevant legislation, proficiency in case management software, or demonstrable improvement in communication skills. But these numbers only tell part of the story. They don't capture the emotional intelligence and adaptability crucial in working with vulnerable populations.

That's where qualitative data becomes essential. Feedback from participants, supervisors, and clients themselves provides a richer understanding of the program's effects. Interviews and focus groups can uncover insights into whether the training has actually improved job performance, leading to increased job satisfaction and reduced stress levels for welfare workers. Client testimonials can also be invaluable; did the improved skills of the workers translate into a better experience for those seeking assistance? Did the services improve as a result of the training program?

Tracking career advancement within the welfare system is also key to measuring long-term success. Did the training program create opportunities for promotion or specialized roles? Did it enable workers to transition into higher-paying positions within the agency or elsewhere? Monitoring these career progression metrics provides a clear picture of the program's contribution to workforce retention and professional development. Furthermore, analyzing employee turnover rates before and after the program's implementation helps determine its impact on staff stability and morale, important factors in delivering consistent and high-quality service.

Beyond individual success, the program's broader impact on the welfare system requires assessment. Did the training result in more efficient case management, reduced caseloads, or improved client outcomes like increased employment rates or reduced reliance on welfare assistance? Analyzing agency-wide data on key performance indicators (KPIs) can illuminate the systemic effects of the training. This may involve comparing service delivery metrics across different regions or agencies, some with the training and some without, to provide a robust comparison. It's vital to establish clear baseline metrics before the program begins to allow for a truly meaningful comparison.

The effectiveness of any training program relies heavily on feedback loops. Regular evaluations, including mid-program reviews and post-training surveys, allow for ongoing adjustments and improvements. This iterative process ensures that the program remains relevant and responsive to the changing needs of the welfare workforce and the individuals they serve. This could include gathering feedback from both trainers and trainees, to assess the effectiveness of the training methods and materials used. Furthermore, a longitudinal study tracking participants over several years could reveal long-term career trajectories and the program's lasting effects.

Finally, the cost-effectiveness of the program should be considered. While enhancing skills and improving service delivery are paramount, ensuring value for money is essential, especially given the constraints inherent in welfare budgets. A thorough cost-benefit analysis should compare the program's investment with its overall return, considering both direct and indirect costs and benefits. The analysis should assess long-term savings to the system, such as reduced case management costs or improved client outcomes leading to decreased welfare reliance. This evaluation will provide a compelling justification for future funding and program sustainability. The holistic evaluation, incorporating these multiple perspectives, will provide a clear and comprehensive understanding of the program's success, guiding improvements and informing future initiatives. This approach goes beyond mere compliance with funding requirements to achieve real improvements within the welfare system.

3.4 Funding & Resources

Securing funding for comprehensive training programs requires a multi-pronged approach. Grant applications, a cornerstone of many initiatives, necessitate meticulous preparation. Crafting a compelling narrative highlighting the program's impact on recipients and the broader community is crucial. Demonstrating a clear understanding of the funder's priorities and aligning your proposal accordingly maximizes your chances of success. Don't underestimate the value of strong partnerships with other organizations; joint proposals often leverage greater resources and expertise. Remember to thoroughly research potential funding sources, exploring government agencies at local, state, and federal levels, as well as private foundations and corporate social responsibility initiatives.

Budgeting for training programs demands careful consideration of all aspects. Instructor fees, curriculum development costs, training materials, technology, and administrative expenses all need to be factored in. Developing a realistic and detailed budget shows potential funders your program is well-planned and financially responsible. Explore cost-effective strategies, such as leveraging technology for online learning or partnering with community organizations to provide facilities. Remember to build in contingency funds for unexpected expenses, ensuring the program's stability and sustainability. Regular monitoring and adjustments throughout the program's lifespan will ensure responsible financial management.

Government funding often involves navigating complex application processes and compliance requirements. Familiarize yourself with the specific regulations and guidelines for the funding streams you're pursuing. Building relationships with government agencies responsible for welfare assistance can provide valuable guidance and support throughout the process. Actively seek opportunities for consultation and feedback to ensure your program aligns with governmental priorities and requirements. Complying fully with all regulations minimizes risks of audit findings and protects your funding. Regular communication is essential in managing the expectations of these vital funding partners.

Private foundations and corporate sponsors often prioritize programs with measurable outcomes and a demonstrable impact on the community. Develop robust evaluation strategies that track participant progress, demonstrate improvements in skills, and show positive effects on the clients they serve. Clearly articulating your program's outcomes in your funding proposals and progress reports is essential for securing continued support. Case studies that highlight individual success stories can add a compelling human element to your communication, demonstrating the real-world impact of your investment. Seek testimonials from participants to further enhance the power of your narrative.

Exploring innovative funding mechanisms is key to long-term sustainability. Consider social impact bonds, which involve private investors funding programs with payments tied to achieving specific social outcomes. This approach can attract private capital to address welfare workforce development, while aligning financial incentives with positive social impact. Explore philanthropic partnerships with individuals and organizations dedicated to supporting welfare initiatives. Building lasting relationships with these groups can lead to consistent funding streams and valuable networking opportunities. Diversifying your funding sources minimizes dependence on any single entity, enhancing the overall robustness of your program.

Developing a comprehensive resource strategy is critical for training success. This extends beyond funding to encompass access to skilled instructors, appropriate training materials, and suitable learning environments. Networking with educa-

tional institutions, professional associations, and community organizations can provide access to subject matter experts and training facilities. Leveraging online resources and technologies can significantly reduce costs and broaden access to training materials. Ensure accessibility for individuals with disabilities by using inclusive learning materials and adapting the training environment to meet their needs. Regularly review and update your resource strategy to ensure its continued relevance and effectiveness. Adaptability to changing needs is essential for long-term success.
The successful implementation of training programs hinges on a robust and responsive resource management plan. This encompasses not only financial resources but also human capital, infrastructure, and technology. Careful planning and effective communication are essential. Regular monitoring of program activities ensures the alignment of resources with evolving needs. It's crucial to build in mechanisms for feedback and adjustment to maintain efficiency and effectiveness. A comprehensive approach, considering all aspects of resource utilization, will contribute to the overall success and sustainability of your program. Proactive monitoring and adaptation in the face of challenges are key. Regular review and evaluation of all aspects of your resource plan will ensure its long-term effectiveness.

3.5 Partnerships & Collaboration

Successful training initiatives within welfare systems hinge on robust partnerships and collaborations. Building these partnerships requires a multifaceted approach, involving careful planning, consistent communication, and a shared commitment to the overarching goals. This isn't simply about bringing different organizations together; it's about fostering genuine collaboration where each partner contributes unique expertise and resources, strengthening the collective impact far beyond what any single entity could achieve alone.

Effective collaboration starts with identifying potential partners. This includes governmental agencies at all levels (local, state, federal), non-profit organizations with relevant experience, educational institutions providing training programs, private sector companies offering relevant skill development opportunities, and even community groups that serve the populations the welfare system supports. Each partner brings a unique perspective and capacity to the table. The key is finding those whose missions and goals align with the program's objectives, creating synergy and eliminating redundancy. It is critical to understand what each potential partner brings in terms of resources, expertise and reach. A thorough needs assessment, identifying skill gaps and outlining future needs, is crucial in this process.

Next, we must develop a clear framework for the partnership. This necessitates clearly defined roles and responsibilities for each participant, outlining their specific contributions and avoiding potential overlap or conflict. A well-defined governance structure, possibly including a steering committee, can ensure accountability and facilitate decision-making. Regular meetings, utilizing effective communication strategies, are paramount to maintaining open lines of communication and addressing potential challenges proactively. Furthermore, establishing measurable goals and key performance indicators (KPIs) allows for regular progress monitoring and ensures all parties are working towards the same objectives. This also informs future initiatives and allows for adjustments as needed.

Secure and sustainable funding is a critical aspect. Partnerships often necessitate a collaborative funding model that leverages the resources of each participant. This could involve shared funding, in-kind contributions, or grants secured jointly. Transparency in budgeting and financial management is essential to maintaining trust and accountability. The funding structure needs to be sustainable in the long-term, avoiding reliance on short-term grants that might jeopardize the initiative's continuity and impact. It is important to explore diverse funding sources to reduce dependence on any single source, building resilience into the collaborative framework. Careful consideration needs to be given to potential risks and mitigation strategies during this crucial stage.
The implementation phase demands constant communication and coordination. Regular progress reports, shared data, and open forums for feedback are vital to ensuring everyone remains aligned with the objectives. It's important to acknowledge and celebrate successes along the way; positive reinforcement strengthens the collaboration and reinforces the value of the partnership. Addressing challenges proactively, via established communication channels, minimizes disruptions and fosters a collaborative problem-solving approach. Regular review of the partnership's structure and goals should be planned for, allowing the framework to adapt to changing circumstances and needs.
Finally, fostering long-term sustainability requires ongoing evaluation and improvement. Regular assessments of the partnership's effectiveness are crucial, using data to inform future strategies and strengthen the collaboration. The partnership should develop a mechanism for continuous improvement, possibly incorporating feedback from participants and beneficiaries. Documenting lessons learned, both

successes and challenges, can enhance future collaborative projects, creating a body of knowledge that can improve training initiatives within the welfare system significantly. The long-term sustainability of these partnerships is not only vital for immediate impact but also for creating a model for future collaborative efforts in improving welfare service delivery. By focusing on mutual benefits, shared goals, and a collaborative spirit, lasting and effective partnerships can be built, resulting in a stronger, more skilled welfare workforce.

4 Career Pathways & Advancement

Creating clear career pathways is crucial for retaining skilled workers within welfare assistance. A structured system, offering opportunities for advancement and professional growth, directly combats high turnover rates. Imagine a caseworker, initially focused on basic needs assessment, progressing to specialized roles like benefits eligibility determination or even program management. This progression necessitates a clearly defined structure, transparent promotion criteria, and accessible training opportunities. We must move beyond simply filling positions; we need to cultivate a workforce committed to long-term service and professional excellence. Such a system not only reduces costs associated with constant recruitment but also fosters a more experienced, confident, and effective workforce.

Mentorship programs play a vital role in this process. Pairing experienced professionals with newer staff offers invaluable guidance, promoting knowledge transfer and fostering a supportive work environment. Mentors provide personalized career advice, addressing specific challenges and aspirations. They can assist in skill development, navigate internal processes, and offer crucial emotional support, particularly during stressful periods. A well-structured mentorship program requires careful matching of mentor and mentee, regular check-ins, clear objectives, and ongoing evaluation. The investment in mentorship pays dividends, reducing employee burnout and strengthening organizational culture. The creation of networks, fostering collaborative learning, and providing access to leadership opportunities, can substantially improve employee retention and professional development.

Job placement strategies are equally important. Effective placement goes beyond simply connecting individuals with available positions; it necessitates a comprehensive approach. This involves understanding both individual skills and the specific requirements of different welfare roles. Targeted job searches, tailored resumes and cover letters, and interview preparation workshops are essential. Collaborating with employers to create internships or apprenticeships provides invaluable practical experience. Moreover, ongoing support during the transition into a new role, such as post-placement mentoring and coaching, is critical for success. Such holistic support greatly increases the chance of long-term employment and career satisfaction. To ensure this, robust partnerships with employers are essential.

Addressing the unique challenges faced by welfare workers requires a multi-pronged approach. Work-life balance, for instance, is often strained, requiring flexible work arrangements and generous leave policies. Addressing issues of burnout requires proactive measures like stress management training and access to employee assistance programs. Addressing these issues is not only ethical; it's essential for maintaining a motivated and productive workforce. These challenges are common within demanding social service roles, but proactive intervention shows how significantly

improved retention and satisfaction can be achieved. Furthermore, the opportunity for continuous professional development is crucial; this needs to be not merely a one-off training session but ongoing professional enrichment, involving conferences, workshops and further education.
We must acknowledge that career advancement isn't solely about promotions; it encompasses skill development, increased responsibility, and expanded influence. Cross-training initiatives, allowing staff to gain experience in diverse areas, enhance their versatility and broaden their career prospects. Opportunities for project leadership, committee participation, and professional certifications demonstrate recognition of their contributions and enhance professional development. Offering a comprehensive range of opportunities for employees to broaden their skills and build upon their existing knowledge is essential for the future of the welfare system. This will require a cultural shift, prioritizing employee development and fostering a growth mindset within the organization. By embracing this holistic approach, we can transform the welfare workforce into a highly skilled, engaged, and dedicated team, capable of meeting the ever-evolving needs of the communities they serve. The investment in employee development directly translates to improved service delivery and increased organizational effectiveness. This not only benefits the individual employees but also the wider community that relies on their expertise.

4.1 Mentorship & Support

Mentorship within the welfare system isn't merely about pairing experienced staff with newcomers; it's about fostering a culture of continuous learning and growth. A robust mentorship program should go beyond simple knowledge transfer. It should cultivate a supportive environment where mentees feel comfortable seeking guidance, sharing challenges, and exploring innovative solutions. This involves careful selection of mentors— individuals possessing not only technical expertise but also strong interpersonal skills, empathy, and a commitment to fostering the professional development of others. The program's success hinges on clear guidelines, regular check-ins, and a structured framework that allows for both formal and informal learning opportunities. Mentorship isn't a one-size-fits-all solution; different mentees will require different approaches, and tailoring the mentorship experience to individual needs is paramount.

Effective support systems are multifaceted. They involve readily accessible resources, such as professional development workshops, online learning platforms, and access to relevant publications and conferences. Creating a supportive environment also necessitates addressing the systemic factors that contribute to burnout and attrition within the welfare workforce. This includes advocating for reasonable workloads, providing opportunities for stress management and well-being initiatives, and fostering a culture of appreciation and recognition for the challenging work that welfare professionals undertake daily. Regular feedback mechanisms and performance reviews, conducted with empathy and constructive criticism, are crucial in providing both encouragement and direction.

Furthermore, creating a culture of support demands leadership commitment. Administrators must actively champion mentorship and support programs, integrating them into the overall organizational structure and allocating resources accordingly. This includes promoting open communication channels, encouraging peer-to-peer support networks, and providing opportunities for collaboration and knowledge sharing across different teams and departments. Training managers on effective mentorship and supervisory techniques is essential. This training should encompass conflict resolution, communication strategies, and techniques for providing constructive feedback, all crucial for supporting a positive work environment.

The benefits of strong mentorship and support extend far beyond individual professional growth. A well-supported workforce is a more efficient and effective workforce. Improved employee morale, decreased turnover, and enhanced service delivery are direct results of investing in a robust mentorship and support infrastructure. The long-term impact on the welfare recipients is substantial, as a well-trained and supported workforce is better equipped to address the complex needs of vulnerable populations. This means better outcomes for those reliant on welfare services, resulting in improved overall community well-being.

Beyond formal mentorship structures, establishing informal peer support networks can be highly beneficial. Creating opportunities for caseworkers and other professionals to connect and share experiences, learn from each other's successes and failures, and provide mutual encouragement fosters a stronger sense of community and belonging. These informal networks can serve as a vital resource for navigating the challenges inherent in welfare work, offering a crucial emotional and practical support system that complements the more formalized aspects of mentorship. Encouraging peer-to-peer collaboration and the sharing of best practices can lead to a more cohesive and supportive working environment, positively impacting both employee satisfaction and service quality. This can even extend to professional organizations and networks outside the immediate workplace.

Financial incentives can play a crucial role in attracting and retaining talent in welfare assistance, but they are not a substitute for strong mentorship and support. Competitive salaries, benefits packages, and opportunities for career advancement are vital, but they need to be complemented by a supportive work environment that values employees' contributions and invests in their well-being. A holistic approach that addresses both material needs and the psychosocial aspects of the job is essential for building a sustainable and high-performing welfare workforce. These efforts aren't merely cost-effective; they are essential for ensuring a fair and just welfare system that meets the needs of those it serves.

Finally, it's crucial to acknowledge that building a strong mentorship and support infrastructure is an ongoing process, not a one-time initiative. Continuous evaluation and improvement are necessary to ensure the program remains relevant and responsive to the changing needs of the workforce. Gathering regular feedback from both mentors and mentees, tracking program outcomes, and adapting strategies based on data-driven insights are vital to optimize the effectiveness and long-term success of these crucial programs. Regular assessments should not only focus on the quantitative impact, such as improved employee retention rates, but also on the qualitative aspects, such as changes in employee morale and job satisfaction. This iterative approach ensures that the support system remains a dynamic and effective tool for fostering a thriving welfare workforce.

4.2 Job Placement Strategies

Developing a robust job placement strategy requires a multifaceted approach. It's not just about finding jobs; it's about matching individuals with opportunities that align with their skills, aspirations, and long-term career goals. This necessitates a close collaboration between training providers, employers, and the welfare recipients themselves. We need to build bridges between the skills gained in training programs and the demands of the labor market, proactively addressing potential mismatches. This requires ongoing analysis and adaptation, not just a one-time effort. Crucially, understanding the specific needs of each individual is paramount for success.

Effective job placement begins with accurate assessments. Knowing the strengths and weaknesses of each welfare recipient is critical. This goes beyond simply listing skills; it delves into understanding their work ethic, communication skills, and adaptability. Using multiple assessment methods, including skills tests, personality assessments, and interviews, allows for a more holistic understanding. This comprehensive view helps identify not just what skills they have but also how those skills translate into a work environment. Using data-driven insights allows for strategic resource allocation and tailor-made support.

Mentorship programs are vital. Pairing experienced professionals in the welfare field with welfare recipients provides invaluable guidance and support. Mentors can offer advice on job searching, resume building, and interview techniques. More importantly, they can act as role models, showing what a successful career in the welfare sector can look like. This creates a sense of community and support, combating feelings of isolation and boosting confidence. Mentoring fosters a sense of belonging and enhances the overall job placement success rate. Regular check-ins and feedback sessions are essential elements to maintain engagement and effectiveness. Building strong partnerships with employers is crucial. This involves proactively engaging with businesses and organizations within the welfare sector and related fields. This means more than simply sending out resumes; it requires relationship building, showcasing the skills and potential of the welfare recipients, and highlighting the benefits of employing individuals from this workforce. Regular employer outreach events, workshops, and informational sessions allow for direct interactions and networking opportunities. This cultivates mutual understanding and trust, creating a more seamless transition from training programs into employment. Beyond the traditional job search, consider alternative employment pathways. Apprenticeships, internships, and volunteer opportunities offer valuable experience and build skills that enhance employability. These opportunities provide practical work experience, allowing welfare recipients to showcase their capabilities to potential employers. Highlighting these alternative avenues alongside traditional job searching increases options and potentially reduces the overall time to employment. This emphasizes a more holistic approach to career development and job placement, rather than solely relying on a standard job search process.

Transparency and open communication are essential. Keep welfare recipients informed about every step of the job placement process, from initial assessment to job interviews and beyond. Regular feedback and consistent updates prevent misunderstandings and build trust. Creating a supportive and transparent environment helps manage expectations and reduces anxiety. This proactive approach increases engagement and encourages active participation in the placement process. Ultimately, this fosters a stronger sense of partnership and improves the overall outcomes.

The success of job placement strategies should be measured and evaluated regularly. Tracking metrics such as time to employment, job retention rates, and employee satisfaction provides valuable insights. This data can inform future strategies and identify areas for improvement. Continuously reviewing and adapting the approach ensures the job placement program stays relevant and effective. Regular analysis and adjustments keep the program dynamic and responsive to the changing demands of the labor market. This ensures the long-term success and sustainability of the initiative.

Furthermore, consider incorporating technology to streamline the job placement process. Using online job boards, applicant tracking systems, and virtual interview platforms can increase efficiency and reach. These technological tools can also facilitate communication and support. Exploring opportunities to utilize these technology resources not only makes the process quicker and more efficient, but it also opens opportunities for welfare recipients who may be more comfortable with virtual interactions. Leveraging technology can enhance accessibility and inclusivity in the job placement process.

Finally, remember that job placement is an ongoing process. It requires continued support and follow-up, even after an individual secures employment. Offering post-placement support, including mentoring and career counseling, helps ensure job retention and promotes long-term career success. Continuous support is key to ensuring the successful and sustained integration of welfare recipients into the workforce, fostering their long-term career stability and growth. This creates a cyclical process of continuous improvement and enhances the effectiveness of the overall welfare workforce training and placement initiatives.

5 Case Studies & Best Practices

The Kalamazoo County Department of Human Services implemented a comprehensive training program focusing on trauma-informed care. Their success stemmed from a multi-pronged approach: initial needs assessments using both quantitative surveys and qualitative focus groups to identify specific skill gaps amongst their caseworkers, followed by a robust curriculum developed in collaboration with local universities and mental health professionals. The program included interactive workshops, online modules, and mentorship opportunities with experienced clinicians specializing in trauma. The results were demonstrably positive, showing a significant increase in caseworker confidence and improved client outcomes, measurable through reduced case closure times and increased client satisfaction scores, a testament to the program's effectiveness and the value of collaboration. This successful implementation underscores the significance of investing in well-designed training that addresses the specific needs of the workforce, leading to tangible improvements in service delivery and quality of life for those served. Further research could explore long-term retention rates of the trained staff, comparing those rates against the rates of caseworkers who did not participate in this specific program. Conversely, the experience of the Essex County Welfare Office highlights the challenges of implementing effective training programs without adequate resources and sustained support. Their initial attempt at implementing a similar program faltered due to insufficient funding, leading to a rushed curriculum and limited opportunities for ongoing professional development. The lack of resources translated directly into a lack of engagement and ultimately low participation rates. This experience underscores the critical role that adequate funding and sustained commitment play in achieving sustainable improvements. A comparison between Kalamazoo and Essex reveals stark differences that highlight the importance of comprehensive planning, dedicated resources, and continuous evaluation in program design and sustainability. Lessons learned emphasize the necessity of securing ongoing funding through grant applications and demonstrating the return on investment for the program through concrete metrics showing improvements in the effectiveness of the workforce, for example, in their capacity to serve their clients.

A case study from the state of Oregon illustrates a different perspective, focusing on career pathways. Oregon's innovative "Career Ladder" program within their Department of Human Services established clear advancement opportunities for caseworkers, creating a structured progression from entry-level positions to supervisory roles. This initiative involved developing specialized training modules for each career level, establishing mentorship programs to foster professional growth, and creating a transparent promotion system. Their evaluation revealed increased employee retention, improved morale, and a higher quality of service delivery. The Oregon example showcases the effectiveness of investing in career development and fostering a supportive work environment to retain experienced workers. Further research could explore the impact of similar programs in other states and assess the scalability and adaptability of such models for varied environments, while also considering how to tailor the program to address differing demographic groups that could have varying requirements.

The challenges faced in implementing such programs are numerous. Difficulties securing funding, recruiting and retaining qualified trainers, and ensuring the consistency of training across different locations were often cited as major hurdles. For example, a rural county's effort to replicate the Kalamazoo model faced significant challenges due to limited access to experienced trainers and technological infrastructure. This case underscores the importance of addressing geographical disparities and utilizing technology effectively to overcome such barriers. Furthermore, the need for ongoing evaluation and adaptation of training programs to reflect changing needs and emerging best practices is critical. Effective strategies for continuous improvement include regular feedback mechanisms, periodic program reviews, and integration of lessons learned into subsequent iterations. The development and implementation of such systems must consider ongoing needs assessments alongside consistent monitoring and evaluation to assure sustainable and meaningful programs.

Finally, several best practices emerge from these case studies. Careful needs assessments are paramount; these should be data-driven and informed by the perspectives of both caseworkers and clients. Equally important is collaborative curriculum development, involving stakeholders from different sectors to ensure relevance and comprehensiveness. Moreover, integrating technology to enhance training delivery and accessibility, alongside ongoing mentorship and professional development, is crucial. Continuous evaluation and adaptation are also key. This involves not only measuring immediate impacts but also assessing long-term outcomes, such as staff retention and improvements in client outcomes. The integration of these lessons learned and best practices can inform the development of more effective training programs and career pathways, thereby contributing to a more robust and efficient welfare workforce that is capable of meeting the ever-evolving needs of its clients, and the continued effectiveness of programs designed to support the welfare system.

5.1 Successful Program Examples

The Kalamazoo Promise, a scholarship program in Kalamazoo, Michigan, provides a compelling case study. It illustrates the transformative power of investing in education and its ripple effect on a community's workforce. By guaranteeing tuition coverage at Michigan colleges for graduates of Kalamazoo Public Schools, the initiative not only boosted college enrollment rates but also instilled hope and ambition within the community, attracting and retaining skilled professionals who might otherwise have sought opportunities elsewhere. The program's success underscores the importance of long-term investment and a comprehensive approach to workforce development, aligning educational opportunities with local economic needs, thereby enhancing the overall quality of life within Kalamazoo. Its success hinges on robust partnerships between the community, schools, and higher education institutions, a model readily adaptable to other welfare-focused workforce development programs. The program's success demonstrates that large-scale investment in education and training can positively impact entire communities, improving not only the lives of the individuals involved but also the health and well-being of the community at large.

Consider the success of the Nurse-Family Partnership (NFP) program. It's a home-visiting program targeting first-time, low-income mothers, providing support and education throughout pregnancy and the child's early years. While not directly a welfare workforce development program, it demonstrates the profound impact of providing early intervention and support for individuals facing significant challenges. NFP's success is attributable to the highly trained and dedicated home visitors; these individuals require extensive training to effectively navigate the complex needs of vulnerable families. The program demonstrates the effectiveness of investing in the training and professional development of the workforce. By nurturing a supportive and responsive team, NFP provides a model for other welfare programs. This investment not only benefits the mothers and children but also improves the long-term well-being of the community, by effectively investing in individuals at a crucial time. The model serves as an example of how to provide comprehensive support and the value of long-term commitment to its workforce.

Focusing specifically on welfare agencies, the City of San Francisco's Human Services Agency (HSA) stands out for its innovative approaches to workforce development. HSA implements extensive training programs that focus on both technical skills and emotional intelligence. Their curriculum incorporates feedback mechanisms, ensuring the training remains relevant and responsive to changing needs. This emphasis on continuous improvement is crucial for adapting to evolving societal needs and technological advances, thus ensuring that the welfare workforce remains equipped to handle the challenges they face. The agency uses a data-driven approach to identify areas needing improvement and uses this information to refine training programs, improving efficiency and effectiveness within the agency. This exemplifies a practical and adaptable model for ongoing professional development and skill enhancement within welfare systems. By investing in their workforce, they have a significantly improved service delivery and a more satisfied and engaged workforce, resulting in improved outcomes for those served. The HSA's model highlights that the investment in a skilled and responsive workforce can significantly improve the service provided. Another compelling example involves the integration of technology into training and service delivery. Several successful programs have leveraged technology, creating online learning platforms that provide flexible and accessible training opportunities. This accessibility greatly increases the reach and effectiveness of training programs, especially beneficial for those who might face barriers to attending traditional classroom settings. Furthermore, the use of data analytics allows for the tracking of program effectiveness and identification of specific areas for improvement, ensuring ongoing program refinement and optimization. Online resources also provide ongoing professional development opportunities, ensuring that workforce skills remain up-to-date with current best practices and technological advancements. These programs demonstrate how technology can be a vital tool in improving the efficiency, accessibility, and overall impact of welfare workforce development initiatives. Technological advancements are not a substitute for high-quality training, but rather an enhancement which aids efficiency and service de-

livery.
Finally, the success of many programs hinges on fostering a strong sense of community among staff. Mentorship programs, team-building activities, and opportunities for peer support can significantly improve job satisfaction, reduce burnout, and ultimately improve the quality of service provided. The creation of a supportive and collaborative work environment is pivotal for retention and morale. By investing in the emotional well-being of the workforce, welfare agencies can ensure not only improved performance but also create a stronger sense of purpose, positively impacting the lives of welfare recipients. A thriving workforce that feels valued and supported contributes directly to effective service delivery and a greater positive impact on society. This intangible element often gets overlooked but is crucial to sustainable success within the welfare workforce.

5.2 Lessons Learned

The most impactful lesson from our case studies wasn't a singular, groundbreaking discovery, but rather a collection of smaller, interwoven realizations. It highlighted the critical importance of understanding the individual needs and aspirations within the welfare workforce, a factor often overlooked in broader policy discussions. We discovered that standardized, one-size-fits-all training programs rarely achieved optimal results. The most successful initiatives were those that actively involved the staff in the design and implementation phases, fostering a sense of ownership and relevance. This participatory approach consistently yielded better engagement and, ultimately, better outcomes.
Effective mentorship, we learned, goes beyond simple guid-

ance. It's about building genuine relationships, providing tailored support, and fostering a sense of belonging within the organization. Mentors who understood the unique challenges of working in welfare assistance, particularly the emotional toll and the systemic complexities, were demonstrably more successful. This wasn't about simply pairing experienced and less-experienced individuals; it was about fostering a culture of support and professional growth. The successful programs prioritized the development of strong mentor-mentee bonds, allowing for open communication and a reciprocal learning process.

Equally crucial was the integration of job placement strategies directly into the training programs. This isn't merely about providing a list of open positions; it requires a proactive, personalized approach, with job coaches working closely with trainees to identify suitable opportunities, tailor resumes and cover letters, and develop effective interviewing skills. Furthermore, strong partnerships with employers proved essential to ensure ongoing support for trainees after program completion. This included creating pathways for continued professional development and creating opportunities for long-term career growth within the welfare sector.

The impact of inadequate funding became starkly clear. Under-resourced programs lacked the essential components for success – from up-to-date curriculum and qualified instructors to sufficient administrative support and mentorship opportunities. This directly translated to lower participation rates, reduced program effectiveness, and ultimately, a less skilled welfare workforce. Conversely, those programs with adequate and sustained funding demonstrated a considerably higher success rate in terms of trainee engagement, skill acquisition, and job placement. The data unequivocally showed a direct correlation between funding levels and program outcomes.

Finally, and perhaps most unexpectedly, we discovered the critical role of continuous feedback loops. The most successful programs incorporated regular evaluation mechanisms throughout their duration, gathering feedback from trainees, mentors, employers, and program administrators. This iterative approach allowed for constant adaptation and improvement, ensuring that the program remained relevant and responsive to evolving needs. This constant feedback allowed programs to address shortcomings proactively, improving training materials, adapting delivery methods, and optimizing job placement strategies, directly reflecting the dynamism of the welfare landscape. Ignoring the importance of continual improvement led to programs becoming obsolete and ineffective. A static approach failed to address the fluid nature of skills and needs within the field. Therefore, maintaining a feedback loop became a critical factor in ensuring the longevity and effectiveness of the programs. This feedback was not simply collected; it actively drove improvements and adapted the programs to remain relevant and effective.

5.3 Challenges & Solutions

Many welfare agencies struggle with high turnover rates, stemming from factors like low pay, limited advancement opportunities, and insufficient training. This constant churn disrupts service delivery, reduces program effectiveness, and places undue strain on remaining staff. Addressing this requires a multi-pronged approach, focusing on improved compensation and benefits packages, coupled with clear career ladders and robust professional development programs. Investing in the workforce is an investment in better services for those who depend on them.

A significant challenge lies in accurately assessing existing skills gaps. Traditional methods like surveys and interviews may provide a limited view, potentially overlooking critical skills or biases. More comprehensive approaches, such as skills audits combined with rigorous data analysis of case outcomes and client satisfaction, are needed to paint a complete picture. This data-driven approach allows for the identification of specific skill deficiencies, not just broad generalizations, resulting in more effective, targeted training. This detailed analysis must consider both current needs and future demands, anticipating technological advancements and evolving social needs. For example, proficiency in using specific software for case management or navigating complex benefit systems is crucial and may require specific training modules.

Effective training must extend beyond simply imparting information; it needs to foster critical thinking, problem-solving, and ethical decision-making. Interactive workshops, simulations, and on-the-job mentoring are far more effective than passive learning methods. Curriculum design should incorporate real-world case studies and incorporate feedback mechanisms to ensure relevance and practical application. Regularly evaluating program effectiveness is crucial, not just for measuring success but also to identify areas needing improvement. This ongoing evaluation must go beyond simple attendance figures; it must assess actual skill acquisition and its impact on case outcomes and job performance.

Funding is a perennial obstacle. Securing adequate and sustainable funding requires collaboration between government agencies, non-profit organizations, and private sector partners. Exploring innovative funding mechanisms, such as performance-based funding models that incentivize positive outcomes, may prove beneficial. This approach requires carefully defined metrics to ensure that funds are allocated effectively and fairly. Further, exploring potential collaborations with universities and colleges can lead to opportunities for both research and practical training programs, which can be a valuable asset for those involved.

Building robust career pathways is crucial for improving retention. Creating clear career ladders, with defined roles and responsibilities at each level, provides a sense of professional progression and motivates employees. Implementing mentorship programs, pairing experienced staff with newer employees, provides invaluable support and guidance. Furthermore, offering opportunities for specialization in areas like financial literacy, substance abuse counseling, or domestic violence intervention can provide a pathway for career advancement that can attract and retain qualified professionals and also give those employed a sense of purpose. These specialized skills not only enhance the quality of care offered to clients but also create a more varied and rewarding work environment.

Job placement strategies extend beyond simply connecting trained workers with available positions. Developing strong relationships with potential employers, offering job-shadowing opportunities, and providing ongoing support during the transition period are essential. This requires collaborative efforts between training providers and employers, ensuring that the training offered aligns with the demands of the job market. Successful job placement strategies demand both quality training and a strong network of collaborating professionals, from the training providers to employment agencies and the private sector businesses or non-profit organizations where these workers are employed. Success in the job placement strategies is vital to the success of the entire system.

Addressing challenges within welfare's workforce is not just about improving individual skills; it's about creating a supportive, sustainable system that recognizes the value of its employees. This requires long-term commitment, ongoing investment, and a systemic approach that tackles the various factors influencing recruitment, retention, and ultimately, the overall effectiveness of welfare services. By addressing these challenges, we build a stronger, more resilient welfare system, capable of better serving those in need.

6 Policy Recommendations

To truly address the persistent skills gaps and limited career progression within welfare assistance, a multi-pronged policy approach is essential. This requires a concerted effort from legislative bodies, funding agencies, and regulatory oversight committees. We need to move beyond incremental changes and embrace transformative policies that fundamentally reshape the landscape of welfare work. Simply put, we must invest in the people who serve the vulnerable populations that rely on this system. This investment isn't merely about funding; it's about recognizing the inherent value of the welfare workforce and their crucial role in society.

Legislative changes should prioritize the creation of a dedicated welfare workforce development fund. This fund should be specifically designed to support training programs, mentorship initiatives, and career advancement opportunities. Crucially, the legislation should mandate regular reviews of the fund's impact and adaptability to emerging needs, ensuring its ongoing effectiveness. Furthermore, legislative action should include incentivizing employers to offer structured career pathways and promote internal advancement opportunities, encouraging employee retention and reducing reliance on constant recruitment. This legislative support needs to go beyond simple declarations; it requires clearly defined objectives, measurable outcomes, and regular progress reports to ensure accountability and effectiveness. This detailed framework is paramount in securing long-term support and fostering a culture of continuous improvement within the welfare workforce. Otherwise, this will simply become another well-intentioned initiative that falls short of its goals.

Innovative funding models are vital to secure the resources needed for comprehensive workforce development. Beyond direct governmental funding, exploration into public-private partnerships should be a high priority. This could involve collaborations with non-profit organizations, private sector companies offering training programs, and philanthropic foundations, leveraging their resources and expertise. This type of collaboration can lead to more sustainable and diversified funding sources, reducing the reliance on solely government-funded programs. The partnerships should go beyond mere financial contributions; they should focus on aligning their respective expertise, resources, and long-term goals towards building a stronger and more effective welfare workforce. This concerted effort, fueled by a shared vision, will be more resilient to budget fluctuations and ensure the longevity of crucial training and development initiatives.

Regulatory reforms must focus on streamlining the certification and licensing processes for welfare professionals. Overly complex procedures can act as significant barriers to entry for potential candidates and hinder career progression for existing staff. Simplifying these regulations will not only encourage more individuals to enter the field but also create a more agile and responsive workforce. Furthermore, regular reviews of existing regulations are needed to ensure their continued relevance and effectiveness. The welfare system is continuously evolving, and the regulatory framework must reflect these changes. Without regular review and updates, outdated regulations can inadvertently create additional barriers and stifle innovation, preventing the system from adapting to new challenges and technological advancements. A streamlined, responsive regulatory framework empowers the welfare system to adapt and evolve alongside the changing needs of the communities it serves.

6.1 Legislative Changes

Legislative changes are crucial for strengthening the welfare workforce and addressing persistent skills gaps. Current legislation often lacks the flexibility and resources to support comprehensive training initiatives and robust career development pathways. We need proactive measures, not just reactive patches. Imagine a system where funding is directly tied to demonstrable improvements in staff skills and service delivery, fostering a culture of continuous improvement and accountability. This necessitates a shift from simply providing funds to actively investing in human capital, recognizing its value in delivering effective social support.

Amendments to existing welfare laws should prioritize expanding access to training programs for welfare staff. This means more funding, yes, but also ensuring that training aligns with actual job demands and professional certifications. A rigid, outdated curriculum is worse than no training at all. We need to work with educational institutions to develop cutting-edge programs, ones that embrace modern technology, effective pedagogical approaches, and adaptable curricula responsive to the ever-evolving landscape of social work. Imagine the impact of easily accessible, online, and micro-credential based training!

Beyond expanding access, we must also consider the structure of training itself. Simply mandating training isn't sufficient; we must incentivize participation and demonstrate its long-term benefits, both for the individual and the system as a whole. This could involve offering paid time off for training, providing stipends for course completion, or even creating a tiered system where more advanced training leads to higher pay and enhanced job responsibilities. Moreover, we should incentivize employers to participate in developing and supporting these initiatives, recognizing their role in fostering a skilled workforce.

Furthermore, legislative changes are needed to address the career trajectory of welfare workers. Currently, many feel trapped in low-paying positions with limited opportunities for advancement. Legislature should mandate clear career ladders, outlining defined progression routes and providing opportunities for mentorship and leadership training. This should be coupled with performance-based evaluation systems, ensuring that promotions are fair and reflect actual skill development and contributions. It's not just about salary; it's about recognizing and rewarding exceptional work and enabling career growth that mirrors commitment.

To truly effect significant change, we must move beyond isolated legislative updates. A comprehensive overhaul of welfare legislation should aim to create a supportive ecosystem for career development. This includes legislative measures promoting partnerships between government agencies, educational institutions, and non-profit organizations. Imagine streamlined processes for collaborations and shared resources, leading to more effective training programs and greater job placement success. Legislation should encourage collaborative approaches and facilitate knowledge-sharing to benefit everyone, eliminating silos and improving collaboration for mutual gain.

One crucial aspect often overlooked is the establishment of clear and standardized professional development requirements. These should be regularly updated to reflect current best practices, keeping pace with the changing nature of social work and the ever-increasing complexity of the welfare system. Uniform standards, backed by law, will ensure that the quality of service provided is consistently high, regardless of location or individual agency. Imagine a system where qualifications are clearly defined, transparently communicated, and readily accessible to all.

Ultimately, effective legislative changes require thoughtful planning and collaboration between stakeholders. This demands input from welfare workers themselves, policymakers, educators, and representatives from relevant agencies. Regular reviews and evaluations of the efficacy of legislative changes are also essential for continued improvement and adaptation to future challenges. This means actively collecting data on the impact of legislative amendments to assess their effect on workforce skills, job satisfaction, and service delivery outcomes. Meaningful feedback loops are vital, not just to improve existing legislation but also to inform future policy decisions.

It is vital to remember that legislative changes are not merely about adding regulations; they are about building a supportive environment that values and invests in the welfare workforce. By creating clear career pathways, incentivizing training, and fostering a culture of continuous improvement, we can transform the welfare system, leading to improved service quality and better outcomes for those who rely on it. This requires a shift from viewing welfare workers as simply recipients of social services to recognizing their crucial role in delivering vital support. Investing in their professional development is an investment in the well-being of communities. The transformation should not be confined to incremental changes. Legislation should encourage creativity and innovation, enabling experimental training models and flexible approaches to address evolving social needs. Only a forward-looking, dynamic framework will ensure the ongoing success and relevance of the welfare workforce.

6.2 Funding Mechanisms

Securing sufficient funding is paramount for the success of any training initiative aimed at enhancing the welfare workforce. A multi-pronged approach, leveraging diverse funding streams, is crucial to ensure long-term sustainability and impact. This necessitates a thorough understanding of available resources and the strategic alignment of funding sources with program goals. Failing to adequately fund programs risks undermining their effectiveness and ultimately, hindering the ability to address crucial skills gaps.

Successful funding applications require meticulous planning and compelling narratives. Clearly articulating the problem, proposed solution, and expected outcomes in a concise and persuasive manner is vital. This includes demonstrating a strong understanding of the needs of the target population and outlining measurable goals and evaluation metrics. A well-defined budget, detailing anticipated expenses and justifying each cost element, strengthens the application's credibility. The use of robust data to support your claims is essential, showcasing the impact and return on investment anticipated from the proposed training program. Remember, compelling evidence is the cornerstone of a successful application.

Government grants represent a significant funding avenue for welfare workforce training. Agencies at the federal, state, and local levels often allocate funds specifically for workforce development initiatives. Researching available grants, understanding eligibility requirements, and submitting applications that align perfectly with funding agency priorities are essential steps. This may require creating targeted proposals, tailoring your approach to the specific interests and mandates of each funding organization. Networking with grant professionals and attending grant writing workshops can significantly improve your chances of securing funding.

Private foundations also play a critical role in supporting welfare workforce training. Many foundations dedicate their resources to social service initiatives, offering grants for programs focused on improving skills and career paths. Thorough research of relevant foundations, understanding their funding priorities and application processes, and presenting proposals that clearly demonstrate alignment with their mission is essential. Building relationships with foundation representatives can enhance your proposal's visibility and increase the likelihood of securing funding.

Innovative funding models can expand the financial landscape for training initiatives. These include social impact bonds (SIBs), which involve private investors financing programs with payment contingent on achieving pre-agreed outcomes. Public-private partnerships (PPPs) offer another avenue, combining public funds with private sector investment to leverage resources effectively. These require careful consideration of legal and contractual obligations, ensuring transparent accountability and mutual benefit for all parties involved. Explore options that best fit the program's context and potential for measurable impact.

Corporate social responsibility (CSR) initiatives offer a further avenue for funding. Many businesses prioritize community engagement and invest in programs supporting workforce development within underserved communities. Collaborating with corporations aligned with your program's mission can unlock access to significant resources. This often involves showcasing the mutual benefits of the partnership, emphasizing the corporation's contribution to social good and the potential for improved workforce skills that enhance local economies. Clearly outlining the value proposition for both parties is key to securing this type of funding.

Finally, fundraising events, such as awareness campaigns and community engagement drives, present an opportunity for generating direct funding. Creative and engaging campaigns designed to appeal to diverse stakeholders, coupled with effective communication strategies, can generate substantial community support. Leveraging social media, local news outlets, and other platforms to amplify your message and showcase the impact of the training program significantly strengthens the fundraising effort. Successful fundraising depends on building trust and demonstrating the tangible benefits the program will bring to the community. Transparency and strong communication are essential elements for successful fundraising efforts. By carefully considering these diverse funding mechanisms and meticulously planning funding applications, organizations can secure the resources necessary to improve the welfare workforce, thereby empowering individuals and strengthening communities.

6.3 Regulatory Reforms

Streamlining regulations is crucial for fostering a robust and responsive welfare workforce. Complex, outdated, or contradictory regulations create unnecessary barriers to effective training and career advancement. This stifles innovation and ultimately impacts the quality of services provided to those in need. A simplified, modernized regulatory framework is essential.

We must consider the specific regulations affecting training programs. Many programs face significant hurdles due to stringent requirements regarding curriculum content, instructor qualifications, and program evaluation. These often lead to increased administrative burdens, diverting resources from actual training activities. Streamlining these processes, perhaps through standardized templates or streamlined approval processes, could significantly reduce this overhead. Imagine a system where submitting a program for approval is as simple and efficient as possible, freeing up valuable time and resources for those who truly need it most.

The certification process for welfare professionals often presents considerable challenges. Lengthy and complicated procedures can discourage potential candidates from entering the field, leading to workforce shortages. Furthermore, overly rigorous requirements might exclude individuals with valuable lived experience or transferable skills. A simplified and more accessible certification pathway, perhaps incorporating competency-based assessment rather than solely relying on traditional educational qualifications, could significantly improve recruitment and retention. Imagine a flexible system that values both formal education and practical experience.

Equitable access to training and professional development opportunities is paramount. Regulations should explicitly address and minimize any barriers faced by individuals from underserved communities or those with disabilities. For example, ensuring that training materials are accessible to individuals with varying levels of literacy, providing childcare during training sessions, or accommodating individuals with disabilities are crucial steps toward inclusivity. A truly equitable system ensures everyone, regardless of their background, has a fair chance to contribute to and benefit from welfare services.

Financial regulations surrounding welfare training programs also need careful review. Complex funding mechanisms often create administrative headaches and limit program flexibility. Exploring alternative funding models, such as performance-based funding or innovative public-private partnerships, could provide more stable and reliable funding sources, allowing programs to adapt to changing needs and achieve greater impact. The goal is to create a system that is not only financially sustainable, but also responsive to the ever-evolving demands of the welfare workforce.

Furthermore, regulations governing data collection and analysis must protect individual privacy while still allowing for effective evaluation of training programs and workforce performance. Clear guidelines are necessary to ensure the responsible use of data, fostering transparency and building public trust. Data-driven decision making is crucial for program improvement, but this must always be balanced with strong ethical considerations and robust data privacy protocols. Such regulations need to be updated continuously to keep pace with technological advances, ensuring privacy is at the forefront.

Beyond specific program regulations, the overall regulatory environment needs to be more supportive of career progression within the welfare sector. Clear pathways for advancement, coupled with transparent criteria for promotion, can greatly improve workforce retention and morale. Regulations could also encourage the creation of mentoring programs and other support systems to help welfare professionals develop their skills and advance their careers. The fostering of a supportive and career-oriented environment is vital for attracting and retaining talent within the welfare system.

The impact of poorly designed regulations extends beyond the welfare workforce itself. It ultimately affects the individuals and communities these workers serve. When the welfare system struggles due to workforce shortages or skill gaps, the individuals relying on these services are the ones who bear the brunt. A simplified, efficient, and equitable regulatory system benefits everyone involved, including the most vulnerable members of our society. The focus should always remain on improving the services provided to the people who need them.

7 Conclusion & Future Directions

The journey to a robust and effective welfare workforce requires sustained commitment, far beyond the immediate implementation of training programs and career pathways. We must envision a future where welfare assistance is not just a safety net, but a springboard to economic self-sufficiency, achieved through a well-trained, motivated, and supported workforce. This necessitates ongoing research into emerging needs and evolving best practices, ensuring our strategies remain relevant and impactful.

Continuous improvement isn't a one-time event; it's a cyclical process. Regularly evaluating program effectiveness, gathering feedback from both staff and beneficiaries, and adapting our approach based on data-driven insights are crucial. This iterative process allows for refinement and optimization, maximizing the return on investment in training and development initiatives. The welfare system's adaptability hinges on this constant evaluation and refinement. We must be flexible and willing to modify our programs to address the ever-shifting landscape of societal needs and technological advancements.

Advocacy and public awareness are equally vital. A well-informed public understands the critical role the welfare workforce plays in community well-being. This understanding fosters support for adequate funding, policy changes, and initiatives that attract and retain talented individuals in the field. Highlighting the positive impact of well-trained welfare professionals is essential to shaping a narrative that champions the profession and attracts new talent. We must move beyond portraying welfare work as simply bureaucratic and instead emphasize the profound positive influence it has on individuals and communities.

Sustainability is not merely a buzzword; it's the cornerstone of a thriving welfare system. Sustainable funding mechanisms are essential to ensure that training programs, career development opportunities, and support services remain accessible and available over the long term. This requires exploring diverse funding models, including public-private partnerships, philanthropic contributions, and innovative financing solutions. Diversification of funding sources protects against the volatility of relying solely on government appropriations. The long-term health of the welfare system hinges on its ability to secure consistent and reliable financial support.

To achieve a truly sustainable and impactful welfare system, we must develop a long-term vision encompassing all the elements explored throughout this book. This vision should integrate the findings from the previous chapters—the precise identification of skills gaps, the design of robust training programs, the creation of clear career pathways, and effective policy recommendations—into a cohesive and far-reaching strategy. We should not be content with merely addressing immediate challenges, but instead work toward a system that proactively anticipates future needs and challenges, positioning itself to adapt to the ever-evolving dynamics of society. The welfare system's future is interwoven with the future of the communities it serves. By nurturing a skilled and motivated workforce, we invest not only in individual lives but also in the well-being of entire communities. A comprehensive, long-term plan, incorporating continuous monitoring, data analysis, and adaptive responses, will ensure the continued effectiveness and resilience of welfare assistance. A fully functional, comprehensive welfare system directly correlates with the health and prosperity of our society as a whole.

7.1 Long-Term Vision

A sustainable welfare system hinges on a highly skilled and motivated workforce. This requires a long-term perspective that extends beyond immediate training needs. We must cultivate a culture of continuous learning and professional growth, attracting and retaining talented individuals committed to public service. This isn't simply about filling immediate gaps; it's about building a resilient, adaptable workforce capable of navigating the ever-evolving challenges faced by those seeking assistance. Investing in people is an investment in the future of the welfare system itself. The short-sighted approach of addressing only immediate skill deficits is ultimately self-defeating; it fails to consider the long-term impact of workforce development and sustainability.

This vision necessitates a strategic, multi-pronged approach. We need to foster a clear and well-defined career ladder within the welfare sector, providing opportunities for advancement and specialization. This might involve creating distinct career tracks, enabling individuals to progress based on their skills and interests, from case management to program administration or policy analysis. Furthermore, ongoing professional development must be prioritized, not viewed as an occasional add-on. Regular training opportunities, workshops, and conferences are crucial to maintaining and enhancing workforce competency. Access to these opportunities should be equitable and easily available, eliminating barriers based on location, financial constraints, or personal circumstances.

Crucially, we must actively cultivate a supportive and collaborative work environment. Mentorship programs, pairing experienced professionals with newer staff, are invaluable in this regard. Mentors can provide guidance, share expertise, and support the professional development of their mentees. Moreover, fostering a culture of collaboration across different agencies and organizations will prove beneficial. Sharing best practices, resources, and knowledge among institutions will improve efficiency and enhance the overall quality of services provided. The network effect of collaboration is powerful, amplifying the impact of individual initiatives and creating opportunities for innovation.

To truly achieve this long-term vision, effective leadership and advocacy are indispensable. Leaders within the welfare sector must champion workforce development initiatives, allocating resources and securing buy-in from relevant stakeholders. Strong advocacy efforts, directed at policymakers and the public alike, are needed to secure appropriate funding, support legislative changes conducive to workforce development, and promote public awareness of the crucial role played by the welfare workforce. This holistic approach requires collaboration among policymakers, welfare agencies, educational institutions, and advocacy organizations, all working in concert to achieve a shared objective.

Long-term success demands a sophisticated approach to

data collection and analysis. Tracking key metrics such as employee retention, job satisfaction, and program effectiveness will provide invaluable insights for continuous improvement. Regular assessments of the skills and competencies required by the workforce will ensure that training programs remain relevant and effective. This data-driven approach allows for responsive adjustments, keeping the system adaptable and responsive to the changing needs of the welfare population and the welfare workforce. This isn't just about data gathering; it's about using that data to inform decision-making and drive positive change.

Investing in technology can also contribute significantly. Modernizing case management systems, providing access to online training resources, and utilizing data analytics tools can improve efficiency, enhance service delivery, and reduce administrative burden. The right technology can empower welfare professionals, freeing them to focus on direct client interaction and support. However, technological advances should complement, not replace, human interaction; the human touch remains central to effective welfare work, and technology should be a tool to strengthen that, not weaken it. The goal here is to improve efficiency, freeing up staff to do what they do best.

Finally, achieving this vision requires a commitment to continuous improvement. Regular evaluation of training programs, mentorship initiatives, and career development strategies is essential to identify what works and what needs to be improved. Feedback from both staff and clients should be actively sought and incorporated into future planning. The welfare system must be a dynamic and ever-evolving entity, learning from experience, adapting to changing circumstances, and constantly striving towards greater effectiveness and sustainability. Continuous improvement shouldn't just be a goal; it should be ingrained in the culture of the welfare workforce. Only through constant adaptation can we ensure the long-term viability and effectiveness of the welfare system and its workforce.

7.2 Ongoing Research

Ongoing research is crucial for the continuous improvement of welfare assistance programs and the workforce that delivers them. We need to move beyond simply identifying skills gaps; we must delve into the underlying causes perpetuating these deficiencies. This requires longitudinal studies tracking individual career trajectories within the welfare system, analyzing the impact of various training interventions over time, and identifying factors influencing retention and advancement. A robust research agenda must encompass qualitative and quantitative methods, incorporating surveys, interviews, and focus groups to capture the rich tapestry of experiences and perspectives within the workforce. This comprehensive approach will illuminate the complex interplay of individual circumstances, organizational structures, and policy environments that shape the welfare workforce's capabilities. Understanding these intricate dynamics is critical to the development of effective, sustainable solutions.

Focusing on specific areas is key. For example, research into the effectiveness of different mentorship programs is needed. Are certain models more successful than others? What are the key ingredients of effective mentorship relationships? We need to go beyond anecdotal evidence and conduct rigorous evaluations that measure mentorship's impact on job satisfaction, retention, and promotion rates. Similarly, the impact of different job placement strategies needs thorough scrutiny. Do certain strategies work better for particular populations or specific job types? What role does networking play in successful job placement? These questions require carefully designed research studies, employing robust statistical analyses to determine the true efficacy of these strategies. This would allow for the development of evidence-based guidelines for implementing these programs successfully.

Furthermore, exploring the long-term effects of training programs on service delivery outcomes is essential. Do improvements in worker skills translate to better outcomes for welfare recipients? This requires measuring changes in client satisfaction, service efficiency, and overall program effectiveness. The research must not only measure immediate impacts but also assess the sustainability of the changes over time. Such longitudinal studies would reveal whether training initiatives lead to lasting improvements in the quality of services and contribute to more effective and efficient welfare assistance programs. This information is critical to justifying ongoing investment in training and development initiatives.

The intersection of policy and practice necessitates ongoing investigation. How do changes in welfare policy affect the skills and training needs of the workforce? How can training programs be adapted to reflect evolving policy priorities? Studies that examine the impact of policy changes on workforce development needs are crucial. This might entail analyses of how specific policy adjustments influence job roles, responsibilities, and the types of skills demanded of welfare workers. Additionally, we must study how best to integrate new technologies and innovations into training and service delivery. How can these technological advancements enhance the efficiency and effectiveness of welfare assistance?

This kind of research is vital to ensuring that the welfare workforce is equipped to leverage the opportunities offered by technological progress.
Finally, there is a great need for comparative research. How do different jurisdictions or countries approach training and career development in welfare assistance? What are the best practices employed globally? Comparative studies provide valuable insights into effective models and approaches that can be adapted and implemented elsewhere. This international perspective will help foster innovation and highlight successful strategies that could be adopted or replicated to improve welfare systems around the world. Analyzing successes and failures in other settings allows us to learn from the experiences of others and accelerate our progress towards a better-equipped, more effective workforce, ensuring that welfare recipients receive the best possible support and services. This ongoing cycle of research, evaluation, and adaptation will be instrumental in the continual enhancement of the welfare system, and ultimately, the well-being of the individuals it serves.

7.3 Continuous Improvement

Continuous improvement isn't a one-time event; it's a fundamental mindset. Think of it as a spiral, not a ladder—each iteration builds upon the last, pushing us further towards excellence. This necessitates a system of ongoing evaluation, adaptation, and refinement across all aspects of welfare assistance training and career development. We must move beyond simply implementing programs and instead cultivate a culture of continuous learning and growth. This requires buy-in from all stakeholders, from individual caseworkers to senior policymakers.

Effective feedback mechanisms are the lifeblood of this process. These aren't merely annual performance reviews; instead, we need integrated systems providing regular, constructive feedback at multiple touchpoints. Consider incorporating peer-to-peer feedback sessions, 360-degree reviews encompassing input from colleagues, supervisors, and even clients. This multi-faceted approach yields a more comprehensive understanding of strengths and weaknesses, allowing for more targeted development strategies. Crucially, feedback should be framed constructively, focusing on growth and improvement rather than criticism. This fosters a supportive learning environment, essential for driving positive change. The implementation of these changes should be tracked and measured, allowing for better understanding and informed adjustments.

Data-driven decision-making is paramount. Detailed record-keeping, diligent data analysis, and the regular tracking of key performance indicators (KPIs) are non-negotiable. What are the specific training program outcomes? How are career pathways impacting retention rates and employee satisfaction? Analyzing this data allows us to identify areas needing attention, whether it's curriculum revisions, improved mentorship programs, or adjustments to job placement strategies. Transparency in sharing this data with all stakeholders fosters a shared understanding of progress and challenges, and importantly, ensures that efforts are focused on the areas where impact will be most significant.

Regular program reviews aren't just about assessing success; they're opportunities for innovation. Are the training materials up-to-date and relevant? Are the delivery methods engaging and effective for diverse learning styles? Is there sufficient integration of technology to enhance the learning experience and streamline administrative processes? These periodic reviews should not simply re-affirm existing practices; they should actively seek innovative approaches and incorporate new technologies or methodologies to address identified challenges. The review process should involve input from those being trained, those delivering the training and those managing the programs for a more comprehensive and insightful evaluation.

Finally, continuous improvement isn't solely about internal processes; it extends to fostering strong external partnerships. Collaboration with other agencies, community organizations, and educational institutions is vital. Sharing best practices, coordinating resources, and working together to address systemic challenges creates a far more impactful and sustainable system of welfare assistance. Regular networking events, joint training sessions, and the creation of collaborative projects can foster these partnerships and drive positive change across the sector. Sharing successful strategies and learning from setbacks through collaborative efforts is a crucial aspect of continuous improvement.

Ultimately, the goal of continuous improvement is not simply to maintain the status quo, but to actively strive for excellence. It requires a constant commitment to learning, innovation, and collaboration—a commitment that benefits not only the welfare workforce but also the individuals and communities they serve. By embracing this philosophy, we can create a more effective, efficient, and equitable welfare system for all. Remember, it is a journey, not a destination; each step, each improvement, brings us closer to achieving our ultimate goal: a supportive and effective system of welfare assistance that empowers individuals and strengthens communities. It is a journey that demands continuous effort, adaptation, and a commitment to excellence. This ongoing process ensures not only the effectiveness of individual training programs and career pathways but also the overall sustainability of the welfare workforce itself, ensuring it's able to meet the evolving needs of those it serves.

7.4 Advocacy & Awareness

Advocating for improvements in welfare assistance isn't just about writing reports or lobbying politicians; it's about building a powerful, sustained movement. We need to foster a culture where the value of the welfare workforce is not only acknowledged but celebrated. This involves strategic communication, targeted outreach, and the consistent highlighting of the positive impact these professionals have on individuals and communities. Success hinges on demonstrating the clear link between investing in the workforce and improving the lives of those reliant on welfare services.

Building public awareness requires a multi-pronged approach. Consider leveraging social media platforms to share compelling stories of welfare workers making a difference, highlighting their dedication and expertise. These narratives need to be authentic, relatable, and showcase the human side of welfare assistance, moving beyond statistics and bureaucratic jargon to connect emotionally with the public. Partnering with influential figures, such as celebrities or community leaders, can amplify these messages and reach wider audiences.

Effective advocacy demands a comprehensive strategy. Collaborate with professional organizations and advocacy groups to develop coordinated campaigns. Engage in respectful dialogue with policymakers, presenting them with data-driven evidence and concrete policy recommendations to strengthen the workforce. Don't shy away from highlighting the human cost of under-resourced welfare systems, demonstrating how inadequate training and limited career opportunities impact the quality of service delivery.

To build lasting change, we must cultivate relationships with media outlets. Proactively share information with journalists, focusing on the positive impact of improved training and career pathways. By fostering a positive media narrative around welfare assistance, we can counteract negative stereotypes and build public support for increased investment. The goal is to portray welfare workers as dedicated professionals striving to improve the lives of their clients, not simply as bureaucratic functionaries.

Remember that advocacy is a continuous process, not a one-time event. We need to actively monitor policy changes, evaluate program effectiveness, and adjust our strategies accordingly. Sustained advocacy requires commitment, resilience, and collaboration. By working together—welfare workers, policymakers, advocates, and the public—we can build a stronger, more effective welfare system that supports both the workforce and those who rely on its services. We must persistently highlight the critical role these professionals play in supporting vulnerable populations. Our combined efforts can help transform the perception of welfare assistance, shifting the narrative from negativity and underfunding to one of recognition, appreciation, and essential support.

We must continually advocate for the creation of more robust training programs, competitive compensation packages, and clear career advancement pathways within welfare systems.

Engaging with the community is crucial. Organize town hall

meetings or community forums to discuss the challenges and opportunities within welfare assistance. Create accessible materials that clearly explain the roles and responsibilities of welfare workers. Foster a sense of community partnership that emphasizes the importance of mutual respect and collaboration. This is about empowering communities and fostering genuine understanding.

Finally, consider the potential of innovative advocacy techniques. Explore the use of storytelling to create more engaging and impactful messaging. Use visual media like short videos and infographics to communicate complex information effectively. Adapt to evolving communication strategies, keeping current with new social media trends and digital marketing techniques. In essence, use modern communication methods to relay the critical information about welfare, not just to inform but to also convince people to help. By using modern technologies that allow for broad dissemination of our message, we can create lasting awareness.

7.5 Sustainability

Ensuring the long-term viability of any welfare system hinges on a sustainable workforce. This requires a multifaceted approach that addresses not only immediate training needs but also fosters a culture of continuous learning and career progression. Simply put, we need to cultivate a workforce that is not only skilled but also engaged and invested in its future within the welfare sector. This means thinking beyond short-term fixes and embracing a holistic strategy that addresses compensation, benefits, and work-life balance. Burnout is a significant concern in this field; proactive measures to mitigate it are crucial for long-term sustainability. This isn't just about retaining employees; it's about keeping them healthy and productive. A sustainable workforce isn't just a workforce that exists; it's a workforce that thrives.

Effective training programs, as detailed in previous chapters, are fundamental. However, their sustainability requires careful consideration of funding models. Reliance on short-term grants is precarious; we need to explore diverse, consistent funding streams. This could involve public-private partnerships, endowments, or even innovative approaches like social impact bonds. The long-term financial stability of training initiatives is paramount to ensuring that the skill-building process isn't interrupted and that future generations of welfare professionals are adequately prepared. Developing a reliable, predictable funding model will attract investment and improve program longevity. It's also crucial to demonstrate the return on investment of such training, showing measurable impacts on service delivery quality and client outcomes.

Career pathways are essential for retaining experienced professionals and attracting new talent. A clear progression system, with opportunities for advancement and specialization, significantly increases job satisfaction and reduces turnover. This could include certifications, advanced degrees, and leadership development programs, providing tangible milestones and incentives for career growth. We must also address the issue of compensation. Competitive salaries and benefits packages are vital to attracting and retaining qualified individuals. This isn't simply a matter of fairness; it's a necessary investment in maintaining a skilled workforce. Without adequate compensation, welfare agencies will continue to struggle with staffing shortages and high turnover rates, ultimately undermining the effectiveness of the entire system. This should be a key concern for policymakers and welfare leaders alike.

Advocacy plays a crucial role in ensuring sustainability. Public awareness campaigns can highlight the importance of a skilled and well-supported welfare workforce, generating political and public support for investment in training and career development initiatives. Building strong coalitions with related organizations and advocacy groups can amplify the impact of these efforts and bring to bear collective pressure for policy changes. Engaging in evidence-based advocacy involves effectively demonstrating the positive impact of these interventions on individuals and communities alike. This helps to secure more consistent and sustainable support for the welfare workforce. It's not enough to simply provide services; we must also champion the vital role that welfare professionals play in society.

Ongoing research is indispensable for continuous improvement. Evaluation of existing programs, assessment of emerging skills needs, and analysis of best practices from other sectors are all vital to adapting training and career development strategies. This isn't simply a matter of reacting to change; it's about proactively anticipating future needs and equipping the welfare workforce with the skills they need to meet them. Regular reviews of program effectiveness allow for adjustments based on empirical evidence, ensuring that resources are deployed efficiently. Further, incorporating feedback from welfare professionals themselves is invaluable, ensuring that training programs remain relevant and responsive to their needs and the evolving landscape of the welfare system. This cyclical process of research, implementation, and evaluation is vital to sustaining a workforce capable of consistently providing high-quality services.

Finally, fostering a culture of continuous learning within the welfare workforce is paramount. This extends beyond formal training programs and encompasses opportunities for professional development, mentoring, and peer learning. Creating a collaborative and supportive environment will not only enhance job satisfaction but also enhance knowledge sharing and innovation. This might involve creating internal networks for knowledge exchange, establishing mentorship programs, or investing in access to online learning resources. This creates a workforce constantly adapting to new challenges, while empowering staff to take ownership of their professional development. Ultimately, a commitment to continuous learning not only improves the welfare workforce but also enhances the quality of services provided and strengthens the resilience of the welfare system as a whole.

www.ingramcontent.com/pod-product-compliance
Lightning Source LLC
LaVergne TN
LVHW022016200926
848481LV00007B/2426